1/12

$23 00

DATE DUE

Exploring Earth's Resources

Using Soil

Sharon Katz Cooper

Heinemann Library
Chicago, Illinois

Customer Service   888–363–4266

Visit our website at www.heinemannraintree.com

Designed by Michelle Lisseter
Printed and bound in China, by South China Printing Company

12 11 10
10 9 8 7 6 5

Library of Congress Cataloging-in-Publication Data

Katz Cooper, Sharon.
   Using soil / Sharon Katz Cooper.
      p. cm. -- (Exploring Earth's resources)
   Includes index.
   ISBN-13: 978-1-4034-9313-2 (library binding - hardcover)
   ISBN-10: 1-4034-9313-8 (library binding - hardcover)
   ISBN-13: 978-1-4034-9321-7 (pbk.)
   ISBN-10: 1-4034-9321-9 (pbk.)
 1. Soils--Juvenile literature. I. Title.
   S591.3.K38 2007
   631.4--dc22
                                        2006029706

Acknowledgments
The publishers would like to thank the following for permission to reproduce photographs: Alamy pp. 4 (Reino Hanninen), 5 (GardenWorld Images), 11 (Cephas Picture Library), 19 (Wildscape); Corbis pp. 12 (Richard Hamilton Smith), 13 (Royalty Free), 14 (Martin Harvey), 15 (Hamid Sardar), 20 (Reuters), 21 (Gallo Images/Anthony Bannister); FLPA pp. 8 (Bob Gibbons), 10 (Nigel Cattlin), 16 (Holt/Primrose Peacock); Geoscience Features Photo Library pp. 9, 17; Harcourt Education Ltd p. 22 (Tudor Photography); Photolibrary pp. 6 (Johner Bildbyra), 7 (Tim Shepherd); Still Pictures p. 18 (Jeff & Alexa Henry).

Cover photograph reproduced with permission of Getty Images/Stone (Andy Sacks).

Every effort has been made to contact copyright holders of any material reproduced in this book. Any omissions will be rectified in subsequent printings if notice is given to the publishers.

Contents

Some words are shown in bold, **like this**.
You can find them in the glossary on page 23.

What Is Soil?

Soil is the top layer of
Earth's surface.

It is found on the ground.
Plants grow in soil.

Soil is a **natural resource**.

Natural resources come
from Earth.

What Is Soil Made Of?

Soil is made of broken pieces of rock.

These are mixed with tiny parts of dead plants and animals.

Soil has air and water trapped inside it.

Many animals live in soil.

Is All Soil the Same?

There are many different types
of soil.

They have different colors
and **textures**.

Soil has **minerals** in it. These minerals give the soil its color.

Minerals are parts of rocks.

This soil is called **silt**.

Silt is very fine soil. It is good for growing plants.

This is loamy soil.

Loam is made of sand, silt, and clay.
It is good for growing plants, too.

11

How Do We Use Soil?

We use soil to grow plants for food.

Farmers grow large crops of wheat, corn, and vegetables.

We use soil to grow vegetables
and flowers in our gardens.

Clay is a type of soil.

We can use it to make pots, bowls, and dishes.

Some people use clay to build homes.

How Do Plants Use Soil?

Plants need soil for **nutrients**. Nutrients are like vitamins that help plants grow.

roots

Most plants have roots that go deep into the soil.

Roots take in water and nutrients from the soil.

17

Who Studies Soil?

Soil scientists study different kinds of soil.

They help farmers learn how to grow their crops better.

They study the tiny animals that live in soil to learn more about them.

Will We Ever Run Out of Soil?

Too much water or strong wind can wash away soil.

This is called **erosion**.

People try to stop erosion by planting trees and shrubs.

Their roots help keep soil in place.

Soil Experiment

In this activity, you will look at three different kinds of soil. You will see how much water each one absorbs.

CAUTION
Adult help

(1) Carefully measure out some water into three glasses. Then measure out some sand, clay, and potting soil into three more glasses.

(2) Place a coffee filter in a plastic funnel, then place the funnel into a measuring cup. Empty the glass of sand into it carefully.

(3) Empty one of the glasses of water into the sand-filled funnel. Write down how much water filters into the cup.

Now repeat steps 2 and 3 with the clay and potting soil. Which soil lets the most water through? Which lets the least through?

Glossary

 **erosion** when wind or water washes soil away

 **loam** rich soil made of sand, silt, and clay

 **mineral** part of rock

 **natural resource** material from Earth that we can use

 **nutrient** something that helps a plant grow

 **silt** very fine soil

 **texture** how something feels

Index